W9-DBS-449

Lakeland Fells

Books by W.A. Poucher
available from Constable

Scotland
Wales
The Lake District
The Highlands of Scotland
The Alps
*The Yorkshire Dales
    and the Peak District*
The West Country
The magic of Skye
The Scottish Peaks
The Peak and Pennines
The Lakeland Peaks
The Welsh Peaks

Other books now out of print

The backbone of England
Climbing with a camera
Escape to the hills
A camera in the Cairngorms
Scotland through the lens
Highland holiday
The North Western Highlands
Lakeland scrapbook
Lakeland through the lens
Lakeland holiday
Lakeland journey
Over lakeland fells
Wanderings in Wales
Snowdonia through the lens
Snowdon holiday
Peak panorama
The Surrey hills
The magic of the Dolomites
West country journey
Journey into Ireland

Bowfell

(overleaf)

One of the shapeliest peaks in Lakeland, this is a favourite with all fell-walkers. It is seen at its best from the upper slopes of Harter Fell, as in this picture.

LAKELAND FELLS
W. A. Poucher

Constable London

First published in Great Britain 1985
by Constable and Company Limited
10 Orange Street London WC2H 7EG
Copyright © 1985 by W.A. Poucher
ISBN 0 09 466130 8
Text filmset by Servis Filmsetting Ltd, Manchester
Printed and bound in Japan by
Dai Nippon Company, Tokyo

The Photographs

Preface

In this companion volume to *The Lake District* published in 1982 I have adhered to the same plan as before – travelling from Mardale in the east to Wasdale in the west with slowly unfolding scenes of increasing grandeur all the way. Those wishing to see for themselves the views portrayed herein can follow my route either on foot or by car.

In choosing these pictures of one of the parts of Britain I love best, I have borne in mind three kinds of visitor to Lakeland. First there are the elderly, who perhaps in their youth climbed the fells but who are now only able to amble along fairly level paths: in this book I have indicated several walks specially suited to them, such as those by Gaskell Gill or in Langstrath. Second, there are the tough young fell-walkers who can cover long distances in a single day – such as the ascent of Scafell Pike by way of the Corridor to Lingmell and back down to Borrowdale via Esk Hause and Sty Head. For these I point out those routes which reward the energetic climber with particularly magnificent views. And third, there are the photographers, to whom I give many hints about viewpoints and foreground subjects. My photographs were taken over twenty-five years on Kodachrome 25 and with Leica cameras, the excellence of whose lenses can clearly be judged from the following pages.

The Lake District has long been one of the most popular holiday centres in Britain, with the matchless beauty of its combination of fell, dale and water. I hope good weather may enable visitors to enjoy these walks, but if mist or rain should obscure the peaks, perhaps the pictures in this book will afford some compensation.

W.A. Poucher
4 Heathfield
Reigate Heath
Surrey
1985

Askham

Seventeenth-century cottages, shaded by tall trees, border two long greens in this picturesque little village on the eastern fringe of Cumbria. It lies on the road from Penrith to Mardale, and can also be reached from Lowther Park.

Mardale

(overleaf)

This dale holds memories for me stretching back nearly 50 years. My diary shows that a friend and I drove to Mardale on 2 January 1937 to drink a last cup of coffee at the Dun Bull Inn. It closed down a few months later, was dismantled and was eventually flooded by the rising waters of the new Haweswater Reservoir. All that is left of it is the heap of stones in the foreground of this picture: they were revealed in 1973 when a severe drought lowered the water level by some 50 ft and laid bare the remains of the hamlet. Thousands of people again came to Mardale during the drought of 1984, which also exposed the ruins, though deep mud prevented a close inspection of them.

Harter Fell

Rising at the head of Mardale, one of Eastern
Lakeland's most prominent peaks, Harter Fell
dominates the head of Haweswater. It can be
climbed without difficulty by two well-trodden
routes. The easier is by Gate Scarth: a grassy
path starts to the left of the car-park and rises in
easy stages between Harter Fell and Branstree.

Adam Seat

(overleaf)

Those climbing Harter Fell and reaching the watershed arrive at a gate giving access to Longsleddale. Near the gate is Adam Seat. Who was Adam? A search of two libraries failed to reveal him. From here a wire fence runs in a straight line to Harter Fell, and a sharp left turn leads up to the summit.

Strange cairns on the summit of Harter Fell

Summit cairns are usually heaps of stones, but these are embellished with the remains of an iron fence that once enclosed the grazing grounds on the fell. It has been replaced by the wire fence that the walker will have followed in this ascent. The splendid view from the cairns includes Mardale and Haweswater; and to the south-west lies Kentmere at the foot of the lofty ridge of Ill Bell.

High Street
(overleaf)

This marvellous ridge, occupying a central position in north-east Cumbria, runs in a straight line for miles and is high enough to reveal most of the surrounding peaks. On a clear day, Scafell Pike can be seen on the distant horizon to the west. Where High Street narrows, walkers will see blue tarns sparkling in the valleys far below.

Kidsty Pike

The more energetic walkers who descend High
Street by way of Nan Bield and thence over
Mardale Ill Bell will pass Cove Still, from where
there is this superb view of Kidsty Pike.

Satura Crag

(overleaf)

Walkers who leave High Street bound for
Patterdale, descending by the Knott, will pass
Satura Crag. From this excellent viewpoint there
is a spacious prospect of the wide green strath
of Bannerdale to the north, as seen here.

Boardale Hause

(overleaf pp 28/29)

At this point on the descent from High Street
walkers may rest a moment and enjoy the view
of Ullswater backed by the satellites of
Helvellyn.

Glencoyne Wood

On the road from Glenridding to Pooley Bridge there is a car-park beside Ullswater, and near it is this beautiful wood which turns to gold in autumn.

Fishing on Ullswater

This good spot for fishing lies on the right of
the road to Howtown.

Dovedale from Y Gully

It is quite a slog up Dove Crag, but from the top there are glorious views down into the dale itself, and a glimpse of Brothers' Water in the far distance.

The Kirkstone Pass

(overleaf)

Most visitors to the beautiful National Park will have been over this famous pass, either by car or on foot. Looking back down the pass gives another view of Brothers' Water.

Catchedicam

The north-eastern spur of Helvellyn is seen in
this photograph from the Glenridding path,
which is the easiest way to ascend the peak.

A familiar view

Most walkers climb Helvellyn by Striding Edge, and so have this splendid view of Catchedicam with the path down Swirral Edge descending across its flanks.

Striding Edge from Nethermost Pike

(overleaf)

Having climbed Helvellyn, many fell-walkers descend to Grasmere by way of Grisedale Tarn; and looking back from Nethermost Pike they can marvel at the spectacular declivity that plummets from the ridge.

Easedale Tarn

There are several easy walks from Grasmere for the elderly: one of the best starts from Goody Bridge and follows Easedale Beck to this pretty tarn, dominated by Tarn Crag. It is the first part of a longer hill walk to Langdale, and the drier of the two paths which lead there from Easedale Tarn lies to the right of this picture and is reached by crossing the beck.

Far Easedale

(overleaf)

This quiet and charming spot makes another pleasant goal for older walkers. When the path begins to rise to Greenup (from where it will run on to Langdale) they can turn back to Grasmere.

Children at Castlerigg

This stone circle, lying not far from Keswick, sometimes makes an enjoyable playground for youngsters. Blencathra towers in the background of the picture.

Sharp Edge

The most challenging ascent of Blencathra includes the traverse of Sharp Edge, whose narrowness is perfectly illustrated by this photograph.

Climbers on Sharp Edge

(overleaf)

The climbers are tackling the narrowest section of Sharp Edge. This shot was taken from the opposite side of the Edge to that used as a viewpoint for the previous picture.

Skiddaw from Derwentwater

(overleaf pp 54/55)

This makes a popular subject for holidaying photographers, as Skiddaw is the first mountain seen when they reach the landing-stage on the lake. But it is a long hard climb to reach the summit from Keswick, and in my opinion is less rewarding than many of the other fells.

Reflection

Causey Pike is more usually photographed from
Scarfeclose Bay or with Friar's Crag in the
foreground. Neither viewpoint displays the
mountain as effectively as this one, where it is
seen perfectly reflected in the mirror of
Derwentwater.

Friar's Crag

(here and overleaf)

This popular tree-crowned crag can be used to
give 'near interest' to pictures taken from
Derwentwater shore. This view has Causey Pike
and Grisedale Pike on the skyline. By moving a
little to the right (*overleaf*) the photographer can
include Cat Bells in the encircling ridge.

Flood

The background of this photograph is the same
as the previous one, but the foreground has the
swirling waters of the lake in flood.

Serenity

From the seat at the end of Friar's Crag the
elderly can admire the view and dream of their
conquests of the fells in earlier days.

A view from the path to Watendlath

(overleaf)

The walk from Rosthwaite over the hills to Watendlath is an immensely popular one, and if it is taken slowly the gently rising path should pose no problems for anyone. This shot, taken on a brilliant autumn day, shows Great Gable on the far skyline.

Langstrath Beck

The spot where this study of rock and water was taken lies a short way to the left of the almost level path in Langstrath. Most of the boys in the picture were camping nearby.

Buttermere Fells from Honister Pass

(overleaf)

There are only two good viewpoints on this famous pass: the first is near the bridge on its summit, but it is the second, near the lower bridge over Gatesgarthdale Beck, which yields this stunning view of the Buttermere Fells. Morning light shows them at their best.

High Crag

(overleaf pp 72/73)

Whoever planted the trees round the head of Buttermere gave a wonderful gift to photographers, for their inclusion in pictures of the High Stile range (such as this one of High Crag) imparts a quality of artistry missing in other views from this point.

Warnscale Beck

The upper reaches of this wandering stream make an interesting lead-in for pictures of High Crag, looking here so different from the previous picture. I once tried to jump across the beck but fell in up to my knees – so be careful!

Lakeside retreat

(overleaf)

As the picture shows, this cottage is perfectly
sited, nestling above Buttermere with
marvellous views of the lake and its encircling
peaks.

Crummock Water

A favourite with many Lakeland visitors, this lake looks particularly attractive in its colourful autumn dress. Mellbreak rises at its narrows, but is seldom climbed. From lay-bys below this viewpoint, those arriving by car may enjoy the tranquil view.

Is this
Mellbreak?

(overleaf)

Massively as the fell looms over Crummock
Water in the previous photograph, it is in fact
very narrow as this view of it shows.

Loweswater

On the north side of the lake a band of trees
screens it from the road, and those who revel in
quiet and solitude may park their cars in one of
the many lay-bys beneath the trees and stroll
down to obtain an open view at the bottom of
the hill.

Gaskell Gill

This narrow defile lies between Grasmoor to the south and Whiteside to the north. The path keeps beside the stream for some 2 miles, then peters out on Coledale Hause. There are no steep gradients, so older or less energetic walkers will find it attractive. They may leave their cars on Lanthwaite Green and walk over to the stream emerging from a river ravine to find the path.

High Stile
from Lanthwaite

(overleaf)

The High Stile range of hills can be
photographed from many higher viewpoints to
the north, all of which will disclose Buttermere
below the peaks. But as I was relaxing on
Lanthwaite Green one day, a painter of
Lakeland scenes gave it as his opinion that this
lower viewpoint yielded the most picturesque
view of the High Stile Group. And so I took
this photograph – those who have climbed to
the higher belvederes can judge for themselves!

High Stile from Red Pike

The precipitous northern slopes of High Stile
cannot be seen fully unless you get quite close
to them – as this picture taken from Red Pike
reveals.

The walk down to Buttermere

(overleaf)

Having traversed High Stile and Red Pike, with
their magnificent panoramas of the surrounding
fells and tops, walkers descend by a path to the
left of Bleaberry Tarn. Those making for
Buttermere village will continue over rough
ground beside Sour Milk Gill; those returning
to Gatesgarth will keep to the track above
Buttermere.

Great End

(overleaf pp 92/93)

The precipitous cliffs of Great End, which
terminates the long ridge descending from
Scafell Pike, are much visited by rock-climbers
in the winter.

Base Brown

This hill is conspicuous on the right as you
approach Seathwaite, and its stiff ascent shortens
the route to Great Gable.

Sour Milk Gill

The most beautiful approach to Base Brown starts with a view of two gates on the right of the bridge over the River Derwent and continues alongside the Gill to the footbridge shown in this photograph. When it was taken there was very little water in the stream. Fell-walkers usually prefer the track to the left of the Gill, whether they are continuing from here over Base Brown, or making for Great Gable by way of Gillercombe.

Taylor Gill Force

(overleaf)

This waterfall (which is even more dramatic when the Gill is in spate) lies to the right of a steep track from Stockley Bridge to Sty Head. Sty Head is part of the descent from a long circular walk to Scafell Pike by way of the Corridor to Lingmell: the route is a wonderful one for photographers who could easily use a full spool of film during the complete walk – as the following pictures show.

Lingmell from Sty Head

(overleaf p 99)

This view of Lingmell shows it at its best. Also clearly seen is Pier's Gill which joins the Corridor Route in the left upper corner of the picture.

Great Gable from Lambfoot Dub

(overleaf pp 100/101)

Great Gable dominates the view all the way along the Corridor. About halfway along it the ground flattens out and cups the shallow tarn which is known as Lambfoot Dub. This makes the best foreground for Great Gable.

The cliffs of Lingmell

The Pier's Gill track joins the Corridor (also
known as the Guides' Route) at a point where
there is only just room for the climber to pass a
rock wall that overhangs the source of the Gill.
This study of Lingmell's brooding precipices
was taken from there.

The view from Lingmell Col

(overleaf)

The flat ground of the Col opens up superb views of both Lingmell and Great Gable.

Sty Head from the cliffs

These jagged rocks on the right of the track make an excellent foreground for the magnificent vista towards Sty Head. Helvellyn can be seen on the horizon.

The summit cairn on Lingmell

The summit yields stupendous views.
Descending a short way to the north, the
walker's eye is immediately drawn to the Gable,
and though to the south the view is blocked by
Scafell Pike, there are also splendid vistas of the
Pillar group.

The summit cairn on Scafell Pike

A stony track rises to the top of England's
highest mountain, where climbers usually rest
beside the large but now crumbling cairn. On a
clear day there is a superb panorama but this
picture only shows a glimpse of Bowfell.

Beginning the descent from Scafell

(overleaf)

The track down to Esk Hause is obvious, but every care should be taken crossing the rough ups and downs of Broad Crag before the easier final descent to the shelter.

Cloud below Esk Hause

Once when I was making this circuit I was
amazed to find, as I approched the shelter, that
this dense cloud was rolling off Great End and
affording just a glimpse of the summit of the
Gable. The scene changed rapidly as I walked,
and the cloud had completely dispersed by the
time I reached Sty Head.

Looking down Borrowdale

(overleaf)

Descending from Sty Head, passing Sty Head Tarn, the track reaches the 1,000–ft boulder, and from here Borrowdale can be seen below in all its glory. It is a magnificent finish to this long and rewarding walk.

Rosthwaite Cam

Glaramara, a splendid viewpoint, is usually reached by way of Thornythwaite Fell, but for the energetic walker there is a longer route of great interest which starts at Stonethwaite and climbs Rosthwaite Fell. The walk along the crest to Glaramara, passing Bessyboot and the seldom visited Tarn at Leaves, reaches its highest point at Rosthwaite Cam, poised above Comb Gill, from where there are extensive views back towards Borrowdale.

Doves' Nest Caves

(overleaf)

The usual descent from Glaramara is by Thornythwaite Fell, and by walking to the right the photographer can reach the edge of Comb Gill and this view of the Doves' Nest Caves. In my early days as a climber it was a must for all visitors to Rosthwaite to ascend to these dirty caverns.

The Langdale Pikes from Elterwater

Visitors staying at Skelwith Bridge will find that
a short walk beside the river and thence across
the fields to this pretty little sheet of water,
yields an excellent view of the Pikes.

The Pikes from Windermere Golf Course

This study of the cloudy hills was taken from a
higher and more distant viewpoint than the
previous picture.

Cloud over Harrison Stickle

The viewpoint for this unusual study was the
bridge beyond the New Dungeon Ghyll Hotel.

A closer view
of the Pikes
(overleaf)

Taken on a sunny autumn day, this shot from
Blea Tarn Road at Stool End gives a third and
different view of the Pikes.

Jack's Rake

The notorious rake, rising diagonally from right to left across the face of Pavey Ark above Stickle Tarn, has now eroded so badly that it is dangerous and no attempt should be made to climb it.

Gimmer from Pike o' Stickle

(overleaf)

This beautiful mountain scene draws the admiration of all who stand on the summit of Pike o'Stickle on a clear morning, with its good view of Gimmer (a magnet for rock-climbers) and of Loft Crag above it. Looking down across the dale below, Blea Tarn is usually clearly to be seen, and Esthwaite Water is just visible in very good weather on the far horizon.

Mickleden

(overleaf pp 134/135)

This valley, photographed from the rising road to Blea Tarn, offers a most interesting walk for the elderly. It starts at the Old Dungeon Ghyll Hotel, nestling at the foot of Pike o'Stickle on the right of the picture, and leads up the wide green strath to an old sheepfold at the head of the valley in the centre.

Oxendale

There are several easy ascents of Crinkle Crags,
but the most sporting – and for experienced
climbers only – is by way of Oxendale and
Crinkle Gill. Leaving the car at Stool End,
climbers follow a cart track (passing the path to
the right leading to the Band) and then cross the
grass to the stile seen here.

Sheepfold in Oxendale

On reaching this sheepfold, climbers heading for
Crinkle Crags cross another stile on the walk to
the right and must take great care on the stony
track that follows.

Crinkle Crags
from the rocks

(overleaf)

These rocks are usually very slippery and from
here on the route is not suitable for the elderly.
Agile walkers will make for the path seen on the
right of this picture which leads to a footbridge
and to Crinkle Gill. The exciting climb to the
Crags by way of the Gill (but *not* when it is in
spate) is fully described in my *Lakeland Peaks*.
After finally scrambling up a long scree slope,
the walker will emerge on the skyline at Mickle
Door and be rewarded by wonderful views in all
directions.

Bowfell

Long Top is the highest Crinkle, rising to the
left of Mickle Door. From here Bowfell is the
first peak to catch the eye, with its many vertical
rifts known as Bowfell Links. It can be reached
by walking over Shelter Crags and dropping
down to Three Tarns before climbing the path
seen in this picture.

Bowfell
from 'Solitary'

(overleaf)

This well-known cottage stands on the right of
the road that runs from Great Langdale to Blea
Tarn. Photographers can use it in the
foreground of pictures taken from many angles
to include different mountain skylines.

Coniston Water

The beautiful lake is best seen by driving along a twisting road from its southern end along the eastern shore to the northern exit – a route which unveils changing views of the Old Man and its satellites all the way. Near the end of this drive is Brentwood, made famous by John Ruskin who declared that the view from there was the finest in all the Lakes. It was also a favourite with Wordsworth who had a seat in the grounds.

Dow Crag from the Old Man

(overleaf)

More usually photographed from Goat's Water immediately below, this crag is a favourite with rock-climbers who may prefer this view which reveals in detail its many courses.

Lunch on high

On one occasion coming off Dow Crag I was
surprised to see a party of tourists eating their
lunch just below the top. It must have been
quite a job to carry the food so high – but what
pleasure to eat in such solitude, and with such
extensive views.

The Scafell Pikes
from the Old Man
(overleaf)

Hundreds of climbers attain this popular peak
and, after scanning the view to the south hoping
to pick out Blackpool Tower, turn round to
admire the Scafell Pikes – a masterpiece of
Nature. From here many of them walk along the
broad ridge to Brim Fell and descend to the
youth hostel.

Which hill can
this be?
(overleaf pp 154/155)

Many people might not be able to identify the
hill in this picture, but in fact it is Brim Fell
which I turned to photograph about halfway
down the descent mentioned in the previous
caption – a most unusual angle.

Swirl How

Walkers who continue along the summit ridge
of the Old Man will eventually reach Swirl How
whose cairn has been a different shape every
time I have visited it. This view shows Broad
Slack in shadow, with the Scafells and Bowfell
making a majestic backdrop.

The Prison Band

(overleaf)

This rocky ridge drops from the cairn on Swirl How to Swirl Hause: its strange name may well frighten off newcomers to the National Park, but there are no difficulties in its ascent or descent.

Ladstones

(overleaf pp 160/161)

Walkers who make the long ascent of Wetherlam will notice the remarkable change in its geology when they reach the pile of stones seen in this picture. In the distance is Coniston Water.

The summit of Wetherlam from Ladstones

This photograph shows the continuation of the
ridge in the previous picture, up to the cairn on
Wetherlam. In clear weather an immense
panorama unfolds around the peak.

Wallowbarrow Crag

This rocky outcrop, which appears on the
twisting narrow road just short of the village of
Seathwaite in Dunnerdale, has recently been
explored by rock-climbers.

Colour in Dunnerdale

(overleaf)

It is to the connoisseur of beauty rather than to the masses that this lakeless dale appeals, and a drive through it to Cockley Beck in autumn provides a feast of colour to delight the visitor.

Hardknott from Dunnerdale

(overleaf pp 168/169)

Taken higher up the dale than the previous photograph, this picture shows the River Duddon in the foreground and Hardknott on the horizon.

The summit of Hardknott Pass

These days the top of the pass is seldom as
deserted as it was when I took this shot towards
Wrynose, the distant dip in the skyline.

Cloud over
the Scafells

(overleaf)

The giants of Lakeland look forbidding in this picture, with heavy clouds hanging over them. I photographed them from the edge of Border End after climbing the 500-ft scree slope from Hardknott summit.

Clearing skies

(overleaf pp 174/175)

As I crossed Border End to its further edge, which overlooks Upper Eskdale, the cloud which I had captured in the previous picture was moving beyond the dalehead and sunlight illuminated the mountain scene.

Eskdale packhorse bridge

This bridge is familiar to all climbers from
Eskdale who are bound for Scafell, and is a
good place to take an enjoyable break before the
really hard work begins.

Esk Gorge

(overleaf)

Higher up the fell the track from Eskdale passes through this gorge and yields the first dramatic view of the Scafells.

The stone circle on Calder Moor

(overleaf pp 180/181)

Those approaching Wasdale by car will probably drive across Calder Moor from Ennerdale Bridge, and will see this small stone circle on the way. It is one of several in Lakeland.

Pillar Fell from Wasdale

The whole of the smooth side of this mountain is seen from Wasdale, where the packhorse bridge behind the Wastwater Hotel makes a good foreground. But the other side of Pillar Fell, facing Ennerdale, presents a very different picture.

Sheep crossing the bridge

(overleaf)

The flock trotting across the bridge give added interest to a photograph.

Great Gable from Wasdale

(overleaf pp 186/187)

This is my favourite picture – of a favourite dale and a favourite mountain! The noble pyramidal form of Great Gable is revealed to perfection here, and the bridge in the foreground seems to invite the visitor to cross it and explore the dale – even (if he or she is well shod) to climb the peak for its superb view of Wastwater and the surrounding hills. To me, this picture captures all the glory of the National Park.

Great Gable from Wastwater

This photograph was taken with a telephoto
lens, but interesting as its foreground with the
two seagulls may be, the picture does not, in my
view, rival the beauty of the previous one.

The Napes Ridges

A conspicuous feature of Great Gable, the
ridges face south and are often warm and sunny,
which comforts the rock-climber on his tiny
perch as he waits for the call of his leader.

Wastwater from the cairn on Great Gable

(overleaf)

This spectacular view from Westmorland Cairn reveals Wastwater shimmering in the dale below, as well as the fine detail of the stone walls on the valley floor.

Sunset in Wasdale

(overleaf pp 194/195)

This shot, taken from a viewpoint near that of the previous picture, shows the lake and dale bathed in golden light by the setting sun.

The screes

A unique feature of Lakeland, the screes are best
seen late in the afternoon of a sunny day, when
the millions of stones sweeping down to the
lake cast minute shadows and reveal themselves
most clearly. This photograph was taken at 6
p.m.

The Screes
Gullies

(overleaf)

Situated to the extreme right of the screes themselves, the Gullies are the occasional venue of the rock-climber.

Yewbarrow summit

I doubt whether anyone could identify this peak,
for it was taken with a telephoto lens from the
car-park and shows only the very summit of
Yewbarrow.

Yewbarrow from the bridge

Seen from the dale, Yewbarrow exhibits no
special characteristics, but from this bridge its
elevation is striking and well worth
photographing, especially when its slopes are
brilliant with autumn colours. The shot was
taken with a 50mm lens.

Yewbarrow and Gable from the lake

(overleaf)

In spring the shores of Wastwater are bright
with yellow broom, and the two peaks seen
from this point make an attractive picture.

Cloud build-up before sunset

(overleaf pp 206/207)

This phenomenon is always fascinating, and
nowhere more so than when seen from
Wastwater: the build-up of the cloud masses is
slow, and will terminate gloriously when the last
rays of the sun paint the whole scene red and
gold.